TRY NOT TO LAUGH CHALLENGE

LOL JOKE BOOK

Valentine's Day
EDITION

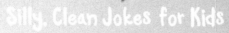

Silly, Clean Jokes for Kids

Funny Valentine Jokes Every Kid Should Know!

Howling Moon Books

© 2018 Howling Moon Books

© 2018 Illustrations by C.S. Adams

Try Not to Laugh Challenge!

Rules:

Pick your team, or go one on one.

Sit across from each other & make eye contact.

Take turns reading jokes to each other.

You can make silly faces, funny sound effects, etc.

When your opponent laughs, you get a point!

First team to win 3 points, Wins!

If you're laughing, you're losing!
(But you are having lots of fun!)

What did the narwhal say to his girlfriend?

I will narwhal love you!

Why wasn't T-Rex on the dating app?

His arms are too short for selfies!

What did the sloth say to his sweetie?

I like you a sloth!

Why did the llama break up with his girlfriend?

Too much llama drama!

What did the unicorn say to his
girlfriend?

I'm over the rainbow for you!

What did the mermaid say to the
merman?

We mermaid to be together!

Where do you find the best
Valentine candy?

Sweeten!

What do you give a music composer
for Valentine's Day?

 A love note!

It is best to love a short man than
never to have loved a tall.

What do you call ants dipped
in chocolate?

Decad-ant!

What did the sloth say to her boyfriend?

I like you slooow much!

Why did the baker make his girlfriend Valentine cookies?

He was hoping to bake her day great!

Where does cupid get his arrows?

Target!

What did Frankenstein give his
bride for Valentine's Day?

A box of Shock-olates!

What song did the pastery chef sing to his girlfriend?

Don't go baking my heart!

What kind of love poems do gnomes write?

Short but sweet!

What did the pie say to his girlfriend on Valentine's Day?

I have good fillings about us!

How much did the fairy love
the pixie?

As fairy as the eye can see!

What did the volcano say on
Valentine's Day?

All you need is lava!

What did the mom pizza say to
her kids on Valentine's Day?

Have a slice Valentine's Day!

Why does the baker love wedding cakes?

Because they are near & tier to his heart!

What cake is full of romance?

Lova cakes!

What did the Easter bunny say to the Easter egg?

You are eggstra special to me!

What is the cheapest Valentine's
Day gift?

Sweet nothings!

How did the pizza pie feel
about her boyfriend?

She loved him to pizzas!

What did the puzzle say to the last
puzzle piece?

You complete me!

What did the cherry tomatoes
say to each other?

I love you from my head
tomatoes!

What did the fungi say to
his girlfriend?

I have so mushroom in my heart
for you!

Why did the fruit tart say to his
sweetie?

I only have pies for you!

Where do people go to get married in England?

 Loverpool!

What did the Dentist do at the Valentine's Day party?

The floss!

Who knows how to draw love?

A heartist!

Where does cupid go on vacation?

Valentine, South Carolina!

Why did the baker give his kids
cupcakes with sprinkles on them?

Because they were sprinkled
with love!

What is a fairy's motto?

All's fairy in love and war!

Why did the boy want to ask the soccer goalie to be his girlfriend?

Because she would be a keeper!

Who did the vampire take to the Valentine's Day dance?

His ghoulfriend!

What kind of flower does cupid like to give out?

Forget me nots!

What do birds give their babies
for Valentine's Day?

Bugs & kisses!

What do ogres give their kids
for Valentine's Day?

Slugs & kisses!

What kind of flowers do chefs give you for Valentine's Day?

 Cauliflowers!

What did the ghoul say to his ghoulfriend?

Be my Valenslime!

Why didn't the banana go to the Valentine's Day dance?

It wasn't peeling well!

Where do computers make their
Valentine cards?

On their heart-drives!

What did Santa give Mrs. Claus
for Valentine's Day?

An icycle built for two!

What kind of Valentine did the
fairy send his sweetie?

A Valentiny!

Why did the snowman want to marry his girlfriend?

Because it was love at frost sight!

Did you hear about the dragon getting married?

He fell in love with an old flame!

Why was the wife of a grape so happy?

She loved raisin' their kids!

What is cupid's favorite ice cream flavor?

Love at first bite!

What do you call a gnomes Valentine's Day party?

A little get together!

What kind of breakfast do horses want on Valentine's day?

Pancakes & maple stirrup!

What song does Santa like to sing
to Mrs. Claus on Valentine's Day?

I Want to Ho Ho Hold
your Haaand!!

What did the math teacher say to
his girlfriend on Valentine's Day?

You can count on me!

Why did the raison go out with
the prune?

Because he couldn't find a date!

If a dog could talk, what would he say to you on Valentine's Day?

I Ruff you!

When do moms have baby boys?

On Son-days!

How did Mrs. Claus like her
Valentine sleigh ride with Santa?

She held on for deer life!

What kind of Valentine's Day gifts
does Santa give his Christmas trees?

Orna-mints!

Who did the fish bring to the Valentine's Day ball?

His gill-friend!

Why didn't the bird get a Valentine's gift for his girlfriend?

Because he was too cheep!

How do you know if chickens are in love?

They give each other pecks!

Why did the skeleton back out
on his Valentine's Day date?

He didn't have the heart for it!

Where is happiness made?

At the satisfactory!

Why was the kitchen utensil not
afraid to ask the spoon out for
Valentine's Day?

It was a whisk he was willing
to take!

Why shouldn't you tell a clock who you want to ask to be your Valentine?

Because time will tell!

Why isn't it a good idea to ask an ancient history teacher to be your Valentine date?

Because they tend to Babylon!

What do you call a cowboy that gets invited to the Valentine's Day party?

A jolly rancher!

This is for the person who invented
sweet nothings.

Thanks for nothing!

What did the bull say to the cow?

I will love you for heifer!

What do spys give each other
when they get married?

Decoder rings!

Why did the spiders elope?

They didn't want to have a
webbing!

Did you see which way the newly
wed computers went?

They went data way!

What did the owl think when he wasn't invited to the Valentine's Day party?

He didn't give a hoot!

Did you hear about the butter getting married?

We should spread the news!

Why did the banana newly weds stay out of the sun?

They didn't want to peel!

What did the poop emoji say to
his friend on Valentine's Day?

Have a stinking good day!

Why don't you need your eyes to
be in love?

Because love is blind!

What do sloths say to each other
on Valentine's Day?

I like hanging out with you!

What did the octopus say to his
girlfriend on Valentine's Day?

You octopi my heart!

What did the fireplace say to the log on Valentine's Day?

Wood you be mine?

What spring flower is a good kisser?

Tulips!

What did the firefly say to his date?

You light me up!

Why did the poodle go to the wedding?

She needed a groom!

Why did the banker break up with his girlfriend?

He lost interest!

What did the coconut milk say
to the coffee?

I love you a latte!

What did the beaver say to the
tree?

I would like to get to gnaw you!

Why didn't the egg yolk want to
go to the Valentine's Day dance?

He didn't want to come out of
his shell!

Did you hear the Easter Bunny got married?

He lived hoppily ever after!

How does cupid know how to fly?

He just wings it!

What do you call a chicken reciting a love poem?

Poultry in motion!

Why didn't the archaeologist want to go on a date on Valentine's Day?

Because his whole life was in ruins!

What happens when your sister isn't asked to the Valentine's day dance?

A Cry Sis!

A clown gave me some sweetheart candies for Valentine's day.

I thought that was a nice jester!

What did the alpaca say to his date at the Valentine's Day party?

Llama just say you are llama fun!

Why didn't the pepperoni ask the pizza to the Valentine's Day dance?

She thought he was too cheesy!

Why do mummies have trouble staying in love?

They are too wrapped up in themselves!

What kind of music do they play for mummies at the Valentine's Day dance?

Wrap music!

What kind of candy do you give an astronaut on Valentine's Day?

Mars bar!

Why doesn't the abominable snowman ever get married?

He always has cold feet!

Why did the vampire break up with his ghoulfriend?

The relationship was too draining!

What did the candy bar parents
name their first born?

 Baby Ruth!

Is it easy for zombies to find
a date?

Sure, they just dig someone up!

What did the fly say to the
flypaper?

 I'm stuck on you!

How can a ship show affection?

 Hug the shore!

What did the corn flakes say to his wife?

Cereal great to be married to you!

Who can marry a lot of wives but stay single?

A minister!

What kind of candy is always tardy?

Choco-late!

What did the gopher say to his girlfriend?

I gopher you!

What can you say about two squirrels in love?

They are nuts about each other!

Why does Julius's girlfriend look forward to Friday night?

Because that's when Julius Caesar!

What do you call two jams who just got married?

Newlyspreads!

Why couldn't the Tin man find a date?

Because he didn't have a heart!

What did the bee say to the flower?

Hello honey!

Why did the frogs split up?

Because it was only guppy love!

How did Cinderella know she
was going to marry the prince?

If the shoe fits, wear it!

Who is the most romantic Queen
in history?

The Queen of Hearts!

What do you call a single vampire?

A bat-chelor!

Why doesn't anyone want to kiss
a vampire?

Because they have bat breath!

Why does a girl deer need money?

Because she doesn't have a buck!

Why couldn't the doe get her boyfriend to bring her out for Valentine's Day?

Because the buck stops here!

What did the firefly say to his girlfriend?

I glow for you!

What did the root vegetable say to her boyfriend?

My heart beets for you!

What is the most romantic vegetable?

Artichokes, they are full of heart!

What did the light bulb say to his girlfriend?

I love you watts & watts!

What do you call two birds in love?

Tweethearts!

What did the mommy bear say
to the baby bear?

I love you beary much!

Where did Frankenstein bring his
girlfriend on Valentine's Day?

The Valensteins Dance!

What did the whale say to his girlfriend?

I whaley like you!

Why did the lettuce back out of his date on Valentine's Day?

He had a change of heart!

What do you call two doctors who just got married?

Newlymeds!

What kind of flowers do monsters give their ghoulfriends?

Mari-ghouls!

What did the pickle say to his girlfriend?

You are a big dill to me!

What did the cat think about the catnip she got for Valentine's Day?

She thought it was purr-fect!

What is a princess's favorite time?

Knight time!

How do birds send each other
Valentine cards?

Tweet them!

Why do skunks like Valentine's Day?

They are scent-imental!

What do genies like to give you
on Valentine's Day?

Hugs and wishes!

What do horses do when they fall in love?

They get mare-ied!

What kind of artist should you not go out with?

A fartist!

Where do rabbits go after they get married?

On their bunny-moon!

Why was the cookie lovesick?

Because his girlfriend was wafer so long!

What do you get when you dip
a cat in chocolate?

Kitty Kat bar!

What is a chocolate pretzel's
favorite dance?

The Twist!

Why did the Corgi & the Pug split up?

It was only puppy love!

Why did the boy bring his date to Florida?

He wanted to melt her heart!

Who had the key to the horse's heart?

The Joc-key!

Why is love like gravitational pull?

Love makes the world go around!

Why doesn't love need a GPS?

Love always finds the way!

Why did the boy take a long trip
without his girlfriend?

Because absence makes the heart
grow fonder!

Why can't a vampire make
a promise?

Because he can't cross his heart
& hope to die!

What did one hog say to the other?

Be my Valenswine!

What did the owl say to his Valentine?

Owl be yours!

Where did the pirate take
his date for dinner on
Valentine's Day?

Arrrgh-bys!

What do mermaids put on
their toast?

Mermalade!

Why did the math teacher give his
girlfriend a Valentine's card?

Because he wanted 2!

Why did the love struck couple
stop eating?

Because all you need is love!

Mom decided to give her kids a new
cell phone with cool apps on it.

They were all very appy!

What is red on the outside & green on the inside?

A dinosaur wearing red Valentine pajamas!

How did the computer make a Valentine sweater?

On the inter-knit!

What color is a wedding?

Wed!

How do rabbits send Valentine cards?

By hare mail!

I want to give you the world!

So I bought you a globe!

Where did the astronaut plan his Valentine lunch?

The Lunch-pad!

Why don't you have to lick the envelope for the Valentine's Day card?

Because it is sealed with a kiss!

What did the banana say to his girlfriend?

You have a lot of appeal!

What did the frog say to his date on Valentine's Day?

You are toad-tally awesome!

What's the difference between $15
for a dozen red roses & $50
for a dozen red roses?

Valentine's Day!

What kind of car does Dracula
pick up his girlfriend in?

Bat-mobile!

What kind of computer is
Adam & Eve afraid to use?

Apple!

What kind of ring did the boy
want for Valentine's Day?

Onion rings!

What should you try not to do on
your first date?

Fart!

What is the best part of Valentine's
Day?

The day after candy sales!

Knock, knock.
Who's there?
Canoe.
Canoe who?

Canoe be my Valentine!

Knock, knock.
Who's there?
Waddle.
Waddle who?

Waddle you want for
Valentine's Day?

Knock, knock.
Who's there?
Mia.
Mia who?

Mia heart belongs to you!

Knock, knock.
Who's there?
Swear.
Swear who?

Swear are we going for
Valentine's Day?

Knock, knock.
Who's there?
Alaska.
Alaska who?

Alaska one more time, will
you be my Valentine?

Knock, knock.
Who's there?
Ben.
Ben who?

Ben waiting for you to ask me to
be your Valentine!

Knock, knock.
Who's there?
Bunny.
Bunny who?

Is any Bunny going to give me
a Valentine's Day card?

Knock, knock.
Who's there?
Muffin.
Muffin who?

Muffin in this world can keep me
away from you!

What do dog lovers want on
Valentine's Day?

Pugs & Kisses!

What did the spider wear on
her wedding day?

Her webbing dress!

What do dogs eat at their
Valentine's Day party?

Mutts-arella pizza!

What is cupid's favorite candy?

Hershey Kisses!

Happy Valentine's Day!

Also Available from Howling Moon Books

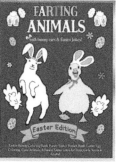